A New True Book

PLANT EXPERIMENTS

By Vera R. Webster

This "true book" was prepared
under the direction of
Illa Podendorf,
formerly with the Laboratory School,
University of Chicago

CHILDRENS PRESS, CHICAGO

Meadow

PHOTO CREDITS

James M. Mejuto—2, 44 (top)

Jerome Wyckoff—4 (top), 10, 40 (top)

Candee & Associates—44 (bottom)

Joseph A. DiChello, Jr.—4 (bottom left and right), 9 (top left), 27, 35, 43 (3 photos)

Jerry Hennen—6 (left), 20 (middle right)

James P. Rowan—6 (right), 9 (top right)

Art Thoma—20 (bottom right)

Abbott Hunsucker—Cover, 9 (3 photos at bottom), 16, 17, 19, 20 (top right and left; middle left), 23, 25 (4 photos), 28, 36 (2 photos)

Reinhard Brucker—11, 40 (bottom)

Tony Freeman—42

Library of Congress Cataloging in Publication Data

Webster, Vera R.
  Plant experiments.

  (A New true book)
  Includes index.
  Summary: A basic introduction to plants with simple discussions of algae, fungi, roots, stems, leaves, flowers, and seeds, and including pertinent experiments.
    1. Botany—Experiments—Juvenile literature.
2. Plants—Juvenile literature. [1. Botany—Experiments. 2. Experiments. 3. Plants]
I. Title.
QK52.6.W43   1982   581   82-9448
ISBN 0-516-01638-5   AACR2

TABLE OF CONTENTS

Top: Crabapple trees
Above left: Water lilies
Right: Cactus

4

WHAT IS A PLANT?

Plants, like animals, are living things. But most plants, unlike animals, stay in one place all their lives.

Some plants live in cold climates. Some plants live in hot climates. Many plants live in mild climates.

Some plants live in water. Some live on land.

Above: Snow-covered landscape
Right: Coconut palms in the Pacific

Where do you live?
Do you live in a cold
climate, a warm climate, or
a mild climate? What
kinds of plants grow where
you live?

ACTIVITY

Look around.

Make a list of the plants you find.

Find out:

Which plants live all year long.

Which plants must be replanted each year.

Which plants shed their leaves in winter.

Which plants stay green all year long.

KINDS OF PLANTS

There are many different kinds of plants. They are grouped by the ways in which they are alike or different.

We have divided plants into two groups—those that have flowers and those that do not have flowers.

Fungus

Fern

PLANTS WITH FLOWERS

Tulip

Flowering tree

Dandelion

Algae on pond

The simplest plants have no roots, stems, or leaves. The two main kinds are algae and fungi.

Almost all algae live in water. Some live in fresh water; some live in salt water.

Algae can make their own food.

Toad and fungi

Fungi live mainly on land. Fungi cannot make their own food. They get their food from other living things or from dead and rotting plants and animals.

Mushrooms are fungi. Some mushrooms are poisonous. Eat only those mushrooms you buy in a store.

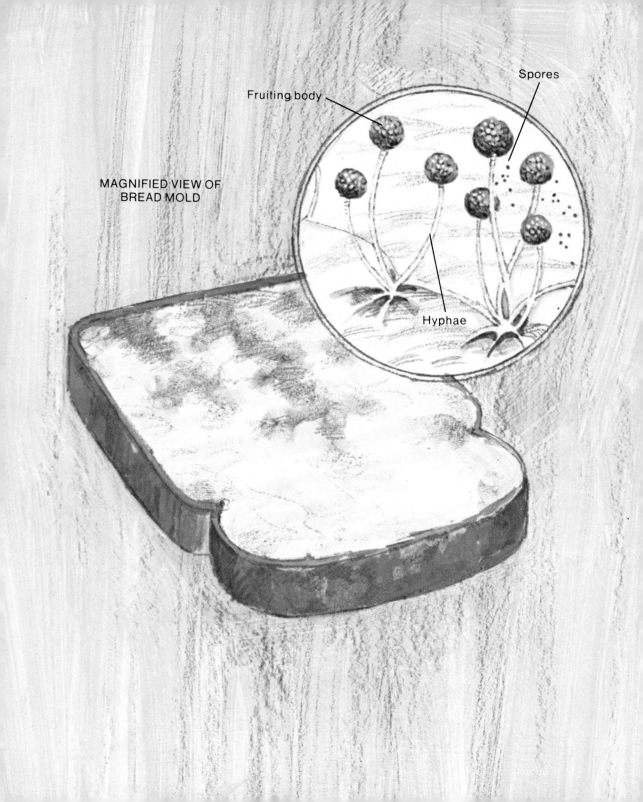

Spores

Fruiting body

Hyphae

MAGNIFIED VIEW OF
BREAD MOLD

EXPERIMENT

Mold is another kind of fungus. It grows best in places that are dark and damp. You can grow some. Try it.

Rub a slice of bread across a dusty surface. Then moisten the bread. Place it in a warm, dark place. After a few days, a white cottonlike mold will appear.

Look at it under a magnifying glass.

Flowers

Seeds

Fruit

Leaves

Stem

Roots

PARTS OF A SEED PLANT

Many plants have flowers. They usually have seeds, too. There are more seed plants than all other kinds put together.

Seed plants have four main parts: roots, stems, leaves, and flowers. Flowers produce fruits and seeds.

14

Dandelion
tap root system

Grass
fibrous
system

ROOTS

Roots hold a plant in the soil. They also soak up water and minerals from the soil.

Some kinds of plants have one large root with many small side roots. Other plants have many roots that are nearly all the same size.

EXPERIMENT

Find out which direction roots grow.

Soak four bean seeds in water overnight.

The next day, pour out the water. Then fill the glass with a crumpled paper towel.

Place the seeds between the paper towel and the glass. Turn each seed in a different direction. Moisten the paper towel every day, but be sure the seeds are not soaking in water.

Look at the seeds every day.

When roots appear, which way
do they grow?

Do they all grow in the same
direction?

STEMS

Stems connect the roots to the leaves. Water and minerals are carried from the roots through the stems to the leaves.

Food made in the leaves travels down the stems to the roots.

Each kind of plant has its own kind of stem.

EXPERIMENT

Buy a carnation from a flower shop. Pick one with a long, thick stem.

Cut the bottom of the stem into two parts for about 3 inches (7.6 centimeters).

Place one part of the stem in a glass of water that is colored with red food coloring.

Put the other part in a glass of water that has been colored with green food coloring.

Let the carnation stand overnight.

What happened?

Leaves have different shapes.
But they all make food for
the plant.

LEAVES

There are many kinds of leaves—large, small, thick, thin, long, and short. Some have parallel veins; some have branching veins.

Leaves are usually green. Their main job is to make food for the whole plant.

FLOWERS

There are many kinds of flowers. Each kind of plant has its own kind of flower.

Flowers may be brightly colored or pale. They may be showy or plain. Some may smell good and some may smell bad.

The flower produces seeds. These seeds can grow into new plants.

ACTIVITY

Look at a flower. See if you can find the parts shown in the drawing.

Tulip

Wild geranium

FRUITS AND SEEDS

The ripened ovary of a flower becomes the fruit. Seeds are usually found inside the fruit.

Each kind of plant has its own kind of flower, its own kind of fruit, and its own kind of seed.

Each seed, in the right environment, will grow into the kind of plant from which it came.

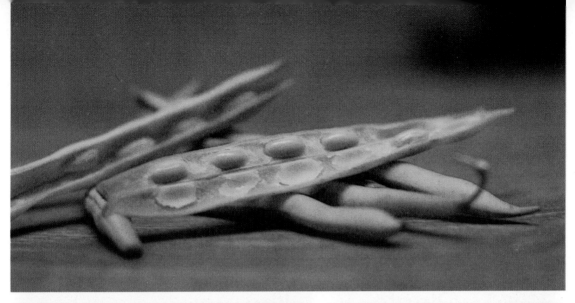

Seeds of a bean,
orange, apple,
and peach.

WHAT DO GREEN PLANTS NEED?

Plants, just like you, need food. But green plants, unlike you, can make their own food. So they need things from which to make their food. Green plants need carbon dioxide from the air. They need water and minerals from the soil.

They need energy from the
sun and they need
something that makes
leaves green. That
something is chlorophyll.

Water plus carbon dioxide
equals sugar plus oxygen.

EXPERIMENT

Get a potted geranium plant.
Set it where it gets sunlight.
Cover one leaf completely with aluminum foil.
In a few days, remove the foil.
What has happened to the leaf?
The leaf has turned yellow because the foil kept sunlight out.

When a leaf gets no sunlight, it cannot make food. Without food the leaf will die. Try it and see.

EXPERIMENT

Place the potted geranium plant in a sunny spot.

This time cover both sides of a leaf with Vaseline.

What happens to the leaf?

The leaf will turn yellow. The Vaseline keeps the air out. A plant gets carbon dioxide from the air. A plant needs carbon dioxide to make food.

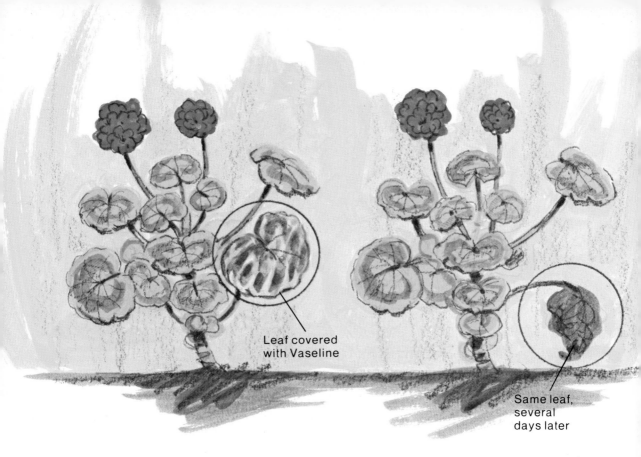

Leaf covered
with Vaseline

Same leaf,
several
days later

When a leaf gets no
carbon dioxide, it cannot
make food. Without food
the leaf will die. Try it and
see.

EXPERIMENT

Get two potted plants about the same size.

Put both plants in a sunny spot.

Give one plant water as needed.

Do not water the other plant.

What happens to the plant that gets no water?

Plant that is watered as needed

Plant that is not watered

When a plant gets no
water, it cannot make food.
Without food the plant will
die. Try it and see.

WHAT DO
GREEN PLANTS DO?

Plants make their own food.

Plants use the food to live and grow.

Plants produce more plants.

Plants respond to their environment.

Notice that all sunflowers
turn their heads to face
the sun. Sunflowers, like all
plants, respond to their
environment.

GROWING PLANTS

New plants may be started in many ways. Some plants may be started from seeds. Others may be started from parts of the old plant. Here are some ways to start new plants.

Avocado

FROM SEEDS

Buy an avocado. Eat the avocado, but save the seed.

Put four toothpicks into the sides of the avocado seed. Place the seed, with the pointed end up, in a glass of water so that half the seed is underwater.

Put the glass in a warm, dark place. Roots should start to appear in about two weeks.

When the stem and leaves appear, plant the seed in soil. Put the plant in a sunny spot. Water the plant when the soil feels dry.

Watch it grow.

FROM ROOTS

Buy a sweet potato. Stick three or four toothpicks into the sides of the potato. Rest the toothpicks on the edge of a glass filled with water.

Place in a warm, dark place until roots and stems appear; then move to a sunny place.

Watch it grow.

FROM STEMS

Cut a stem from a geranium plant. Remove all but the top three or four leaves.

Place the stem in a glass of water. Keep out of sunlight until roots appear.

When roots appear, plant the stem in a pot of soil.

Watch it grow.

Sheep

Buffalo

HOW ARE PLANTS USED?

We need plants. Plants give us oxygen and food. When plants make their food, they take in carbon dioxide and give off oxygen. Animals and people need oxygen to breathe and live. Plants are food for animals and people, too.

People eat different parts
of different plants. Here
are some foods that we
eat. Plants are the basic
source of all foods.

Green peppers

Carrots, beets,
and green
onions

A field of grain

Trees are used to make paper and build houses.

People also use plants for clothing and shelter. Cotton and flax are two plants from which we make cloth.

Plants are important. We get lumber, paper, rubber, medicines, sugar, and fuels from plants.

Can you think of any other ways in which plants may be used?

WORDS YOU SHOULD KNOW

algae(AL • gee) — plants that do not have true roots, stems, and leaves

avocado(ah • vo • KAH • doh) — a fruit with a green or blackish skin that has a large seed

basic(BAY • sik) — main part; essential

carbon dioxide(CAR • bun dye • OX • ide) — a gas that is made up of carbon and oxygen

chlorophyll(KLOR • oh • fill) — a substance found in green plants that gives them their green color

climate(KLY • mit) — the usual weather a place has all year

crumple(KRUM • pil) — to crush out of shape

energy(EN • ir • gee) — the ability to do work; power

environment(en • VYE • ron • ment) — the surroundings in which a plant or animal lives

flax(FLAKS) — a plant from which the cloth linen is made

function(FUNK • shun) — purpose; normal activity

fungi(FUNG • eye) — a group of organisms that have no flowers and leaves and no green coloring

insert(in • SIRT) — to put in

mineral(MIN • er • il) — a natural substance found in the earth

moisten(MOY • sen) — to dampen; wet

ovary(OH • vah • ree) — the part of a plant in which seeds are formed

parallel(PAIR • uh • lel) — to go in the same direction without touching; side-by-side

produce(pro • DOOSS) — to make; yield

respond(re • SPOND) — to react

shed — to lose; drop

source(SORSS) — the beginning of something

unlike(un • LIKE) — not the same; different

Vaseline(vass • ih • LEEN) — a trademark for a kind of jelly made from petroleum

INDEX

About the Author

Vera Webster is widely recognized in the publishing field as an editor and author of science and environmental materials for both the juvenile and adult readers. She has conducted numerous educational seminars and workshops to provide teachers and parents with opportunities to learn more about children and their learning process. A North Carolina resident and mother of two grown daughters, Mrs. Webster is the president of Creative Resource Systems, Inc.